# THE CONTEMPLATOR

Practical Philosophy to Keep
Your Mind Clear, Body Light, and Spirit Free

Vijay Mattewada, M.D.

YAM Press
BOOKS

ISBN-13: 978-0-692-02645-8
ISBN-10: 0-692-02645-2

Library of Congress Control Number: 2014906390



Published by YAM Press BOOKS

Author and publisher contact: yampressbooks (at) gmail (dot) com.

# DEDICATION

To my mother and my father.

# ACKNOWLEDGMENTS

I am eternally grateful

To my family, relatives, and friends

who had to give up their share of me

because I wanted to become bigger.

# PREFACE

Thoughts have come to me throughout my life as to why we exist, the purpose of life, what changes we go through as we face experiences, and as we grow older. A lot of these are about myself- some are about other people, and some about God.

I do not claim 'ownership' of these thoughts. I look at some of these years after I wrote them, and feel they were inserted into my physical mind by a higher source. By myself, I know I am not capable of such thoughts.

I ask you to sit down with me at the level of the heart- not the soul, your soul belongs to God. Not the mind, you are more intelligent than I am; and not at the body level, you have much more energy than I do. It is only at the level of the heart that we can connect with each other.

Some people have a tendency to look at *who* was it that said something, before they look to see *what* was said. My motto is simple. Who I am is not important; what I do, is.

V.M.
2014

At the very moment you are complaining about your life, there is somebody, somewhere in the world, begging for it.

We start with our minds, and end up where our hearts are.

Forgetting the trauma of past events is a blessing;
not remembering the lessons learned from them, a curse.

Err on the side of optimism.

Being satisfied with your lot means not just being content with what you already have, but also being content with what you have left after you have lost most of it.

Faith gives me a more peaceful life than reason.

Every decade, a man is reborn.

If you are happy inside, everything outside looks good.
If you are unhappy, everything looks bad.

When do I feel close to God? When I am curled up under a warm blanket, when I am watching the green leaves sway in the breeze, and when I am ill. Of these, the closest I feel is when I'm ill. It's like when you are unwell, you go sit by your mother, or call her more than usual. She knows something is not right with you. Don't you feel the closest to your mother then? I guess one of the purposes of your illness is to bring you even closer to God.

Learning from your own experience is expensive.
Learning from others' experience is free.

Do what you want to do, what you are able to do, what you are allowed to do, and what is good for you and everybody else.

Most of the time, be your natural self.
The rest of the time, try to be better.

Waiting for an accident.

If you are really bright and working hard and not getting
the results you want, don't lose heart. Remember the
things that were discovered or invented by accident.
An accident may bring you all the glory you seek.
Well, that doesn't really show your genius, does it? It doesn't.
But what alternative do you have—quitting?
No, accidents don't happen to people who quit.
They happen to people who are still in the game.

I realized what I had all along was not ambition,
but a delusion of grandiosity.

There is only one way to lead, and that is by example.

If you died suddenly today, what things would people find that show how you lived? Is that how you want to leave them?

When things go wrong, you can be hopeful they happen that way for a reason. This will hold true until one or both of these two happen—a severe, permanent disability or a terminal illness in yourself; or the great suffering of, or the loss of a loved one. Then, all your beliefs will be shattered. Life, at that time, will seem senseless.

Is there any meaning to these kinds of evils? The only purpose, I think, of incredible sufferings like these is this—that *others* may value their lives more.

We try to understand the world only in terms of what we know.

If you can do something, you have to do it. But if you cannot do something, you are free—you don't have to do it.

The inability to do something relieves you from the obligation of doing it.

What thoughts I fill my head with, define me.

## On criticizing.

Before you judge or criticize somebody—be born like he was, be raised like he was, go through all the experiences of life that he faced, and when you get to the point where you think he should have done differently, *you* do differently. See if you can. If you can, you can criticize him; otherwise, don't.

When making a big decision, always talk to somebody who is older than you. Chances are he or she has experienced your situation and knows more about it than you do. By the way, in all your major decisions, include your parents, spouse, and children as well.

What is the right thing to do? The right thing to do makes you happy and does not harm others.

Don't drive yourself insane with micro details. Verify; don't nitpick.

When a man separates his thoughts from himself, he is emancipated. Man is what he thinks, true, but when he sees himself as distinct and separate from all his thoughts, he becomes truly free. This free form of man is the pure and divine consciousness, the same form that exists in every man, and is part of the universal consciousness, which is God.

The best way to become an optimist is to be around one.

Trust only your soul to guide you—not your body, which is full of desires; not your heart, which is too emotional; not your mind, which always doubts, or worse, rationalizes and justifies your misdeeds.

Don't worry about fame—
there are so many famous people you don't know.

Not being happy with things in your life conceals an underlying sense of entitlement. The fact is that every single thing you possess that keeps you away from suffering is a privilege—one that can be pulled at any time.

If I don't suspend my disbelief,
it is hard for me to get pleasure out of this world.

The biggest credit you are giving yourself
is when you are blaming yourself.

I don't know if God exists,
but prayer does make me feel good.

A 'rational' explanation is in terms of what we already know. If you try to go outside that realm and explain something, people think you are insane. As people would have thought a hundred years ago if you were to hold a small piece to your ear and tell them you were talking to somebody on the other side of the world.

So, I ask, where is the boundary, the perimeter of rationality? Does it keep expanding as we gain more knowledge? Could that be a circle of infinite radius? Why should our thinking or experiences be limited by today's circle, when in all probability that circle is going to be wider and larger tomorrow? Does the fact that you cannot see this circle while some other person can, mean that he is deranged? And just because millions of people believe that circle is much smaller, does it mean those are the true and real limits of that circle?

Are you a prisoner of your thoughts?

If you disclose your work, you seek fame—
even though you rationalize it by the belief
that your work will help mankind.

People live in their own worlds, stepping into
another's only occasionally and for brief moments.
Small wonder there is so much conflict.

Wishing and hoping and wanting things to be a certain way probably indicates that I want to control them to my liking. When I am unable to do that, I try to make sense of why things happened differently. By this, I am seeking to understand things that I cannot control. But even this is not giving me peace. I have found that by giving up both control and understanding entirely, I am finally at peace—to let and see things flow in front of my eyes as they were meant to.

Mankind is also evolving spiritually.

Each day consists of four parts—
morning, afternoon, evening, and night.
Just because one part of the day was bad does not mean that the other parts will be as well. You may have observed this in your own life. So, during the bad parts of a day, remember this.

Try to create a balance in your life.
If you let one area excel, and the other areas fall apart,
your life will become meaningless.

## On real wars.

When we think of wars, we think of a world war or wars between countries trying to destroy one another. But there are three real wars every man has to fight, and these are universal and cause more devastation than all the wars of history combined. The problem is that these are not thought of as wars—and that is why we go into them unprepared.

The first is the war a man has to fight to make a living. Whether he owns his business or works for somebody else, dealing with customers, coworkers, government regulations, laws, taxes, and so forth, is a daily war.

The second one is the war between him and his family and friends. Arguments with spouses, enforcing rules on children, disagreements with friends, are all wars.

The third one is the war within himself—the constant struggle between what he wants and what is right—between good and evil.

Whatever profession you choose, what you will find ultimately in it is spirituality.

The purpose of faith is not to live in heaven after death. The purpose of faith is to live well here on this earth, in this life.

How should you treat people? Don't worry, they will show you how. How? By how they treat you. That's how they want to be treated.

For having benefited from antibiotics without ever discovering one yourself, for utilizing the television and telephone without ever inventing one yourself, for flying in a plane and riding in a car without ever thinking of them yourself, you owe it to mankind to do your material duties well.

You can't get over it; you have to grow through it.

What ascribes fame to people are just
the thoughts in my head.

The longer I live, the lesser I feel that I belong to a particular country, culture, ethnicity, or religion; and greater as part of the whole mankind and the entire universe.

If people contemplated for a few moments that they could have been born anywhere, but by sheer destiny they were born into this relatively good, healthy, and happy life; they will understand that this life was given to them in exchange for a vow they made to their Creator—that if given a good life, they would help others who are less fortunate.

The world is just my head.

As long as your parents did not do anything bad to you,
do not blame them for not doing more for you.
They did the best they could under the circumstances.
If you think they should have done better,
do it yourself and show it to your children.

Volunteering is more about helping yourself
than about helping others.

The range of feelings evolved in man is a limited one—
joy, pain, envy, grief—and all his activities are to pursue
or avoid these things. The feelings of awareness and
understanding, of living and letting live, of forgiveness and
humility, of recognition of each person as a soul with a body—
seem to be unreachable.

How do you blend humility with ambition?

To the atheist in me—yes, it's all random,
but it's so beautiful!

Poverty makes capitalism possible.

Don't be consumed by yourself.

Enjoy the absence of suffering as much as you suffer during times of pain.

We do not look at the sickest, or poorest, or ugliest person, simply because we have no desire to be like them.

Philosophy comes out of the right mixture of suffering and leisure.

Conquer the five evils—
fear, desire, anger, ignorance, and boredom—
in thought, word, and deed.

I'm all I've got.

Those who do not know their fate, will tempt it.

Some feelings are best enjoyed unexpressed.

Should man hold his allegiance only to the things he was born into—parents, country, or religion? What about allegiance to the things he acquires later in life—a wife, a better country, or a different religion? Does clinging to one's own indicate loyalty, or does it indicate comfort? Does accepting things acquired later in life indicate treachery, or does it indicate maturity?

The philosopher who blends his philosophy in fictional characters is vain—he is trying to appeal to the masses for fame; when he could just as well state it directly, but then doing so would confine him to a select few.

The person who quotes a lot is less learned than somebody who applies at least one of the maxims to his own life.

Do not ignore the opinion of you by somebody who lives with you everyday. Nobody can better see you constantly from outside yourself. Do not ignore the opinion of a stranger either, nobody can give you a more unbiased one.

In the past when man was driven to meet his most basic needs, he became an animal himself. With the advent of civilization, will man, when driven to his basic needs, become an animal, or will he sacrifice himself? What about his subconscious? Will it take over and make him an animal, or will it succumb to the power of the will to terminate itself?

Physicians confuse prolonging life with relieving suffering.

Science means finding an explanation for what you believe, not disbelieving something because you cannot explain it.

Philosophy depresses initially, then gives eternal bliss.

Even though the wise man has none of the problems of
the worldly man—greed for money, power, bodily luxuries,
fame, and all kinds of vices—he still has some of the same
needs and misfortunes as him—hunger, need for shelter,
bodily suffering due to disease, and age—and unfortunately,
this is what makes the wise man's wisdom invisible.
The worldly man looks at him and thinks,
"He is the same as me, but just not as successful,"
without knowing that the wise man gave up pursuit
of these meaningless things voluntarily.

Analyze how a thought is going to make you feel before you go through with it. If it is not going to make you feel happy, discard it right when it begins. This is a great way to peace.

People do not realize the value of things they don't have. Not having good looks, for instance, keeps them from being distracted by the opposite gender.

Most people's behavior is due to their underlying stress. You don't know what stresses they are living with.

...And then you are left a body to suffer.

I feel fortunate, blessed to be able to read, understand, feel, and enjoy the things people write in their books.

There are no inventions, only discoveries.

When you say something to somebody, think about how it makes them feel. When you think about something, think about how it makes you feel.

Why do we always look up to the first, or the best, or the richest, or the most beautiful person? There is a desire in all of us to be one of those things. When we cannot see those things in ourselves, we look up to other people who have them. The goal here is not appreciation of that other person, but of the desire in us that has taken shape, albeit in another's form.

If we are responsible for our acts, I blame myself.
If God is responsible, I don't blame you.

It does not matter how I appear, talk, think, or feel,
or what my intent is or my capabilities are—
what matters is if I am actually doing it. Action!

Watch what you love—you may become that, consciously.
Watch what you hate—you may become that, unconsciously.

Believing things happen for a reason, or maybe something good will come out of this, or these pains will go away and my ultimate great destiny will show— all these may not hold true all the time. But embrace suffering—that this life is meant only to be suffered senselessly—and you will never go wrong. Suffering will never desert you.

A society whose legality does not
follow morality will soon perish.

Do you control your thoughts,
or do your thoughts control you?

Know thyself—good. It is easier and simpler to know God than to know yourself. Besides, what is the point in knowing finite and fallible things such as you or others? Spend that time wisely in getting to know somebody who is infinite, God.

Everything happens according to a plan, for a reason—no, not a plan or a reason, because that implies that we know *why* things happen, good or bad—but according to a script, written by an unknown author. We call this script by various names—the genetic code, the laws of planetary motion, and so on and so forth. Whether we like it or not, things are being played out according to this script.

I discovered that I rarely ever get into trouble for not saying something.

Only God is my superior. Nobody else is my equal.

If you keep complaining about things in your life, it becomes a habit, and your way of life.

People give importance to money, fame, beauty, since it seems like they are very difficult to achieve. If difficulty in achieving something is a criterion, how about the task of conquering your fear, desire, anger, and ignorance? Isn't that a more difficult task?

Forgiveness doesn't mean letting go; it means accepting.

Y ou will not win everything. You will also not lose everything. The other option is not trying.

Behind every great success is a great crime.
If not one of commission, one of omission.

Whatever you do repeatedly becomes a habit. Good things (feel difficult initially, but are good long-term) are hard to do, so we never get into the habit of doing them. Bad things (feel good initially, but are bad long-term) are easy to do, so we continue doing them, and finally, they become habits. See how this works?

People are more likely to question nonconformists who deviate a little, rather than conformists who deviate a lot.

Most miseries in life are the result of my own doing (or not doing), rather than accidents or other people.

What have logic, science, and reason done to us? Make us look past miracles.

If a wealthy man showed a child a hundred gold bars, and the child asked him, "Yes, you are rich, but can you do a miracle and show me a copper coin?," what would you think? Would you think that is absurd? In the same way, you look at yourself, a child, a flower, the sun, the moon, and the stars, and you ask, "Yes, but can you do a small miracle and prove that you exist?"

Science can only explain how. Philosophy explains why.

You are either a positive or a negative person.

Life is God's show. All you can do is sit back and watch.

Have you laughed today?

Complain about your life now—
a decade from now you will miss this life.

When I look at a rare and beautiful thing, I want to possess it. I now realize that God has given me the eyes to look at it, and the heart to appreciate it. Isn't that adequate? What am I going to do with all of the things I accumulate? Take them with me after I die?

Do not talk idly about something if you don't care about it—people will assume that you do care. Do not think about it, either, so you will not be affected by something you don't really care about.

Control your actions first, then your words, then your thoughts. Actions are easier than the other two to control, so tackle those first. Slowly, you will be able to control your words; and hopefully, after years of practice, you will be able to control your thoughts.

Be a nice person. It is also important to talk nicely.

It is important to give back, especially when God has blessed you with things. But don't wait for God to give you everything you want before you start giving—it may be too late...

Overnight success usually takes fifteen years and lasts fifteen minutes.

When faced with a situation where you have to pick between one and another, be aware of the other options—both, a little of both, neither, or this first and that next.

There is no original thought or idea.

Humans want to do the best and are doing the best with what they have; but they are, by nature, broken machines. So, the results cannot be perfect.

Hoarding wealth is a sign of weakness.

The most successful people have abundant knowledge and awareness of most things in life. When you expand immensely to have absolute knowledge and awareness of everything, you become God.

Most people read books on philosophy, psychology, religion, and self-help, but they do not apply them to their lives. Really, the authors' efforts are wasted.

Man proposes and God disposes—
but they don't have to be opposites of each other.

Perfection is a process, not a goal.

You are an expression of your genes—
you have nothing to be proud or ashamed of.

Under any given set of specific conditions,
there is only one perfect solution to a problem,
one perfect answer to a question.

Money is concrete, but more money is made
in ways more abstract than concrete.

Actions speak louder than words.
You will also be judged by what you say.

It is impossible to have absolute information about every situation, person, thing, or place. So, go ahead and make a decision and follow through with it. If the result does not turn out well, it can almost always be traced later to some piece of that absolute that was not available to you. But then, it is impossible to get complete information on anything.

When you think somebody is dumb, be grateful, because you are smart only when compared to him.

Take a chance. What are the odds that you will fail a hundred percent of the time?

Everything can be calculated, analyzed, measured, estimated, or reasonably assumed. So, the next time you feel lost in something, remember this.

If you do not have free time for one day a week, one week every three months, and one month every year, you are a slave. To what or who, is for you to think and decide.

A problem cannot exist without a solution.

The only one hundred percent of anything you will ever get is you. Cherish yourself.

Unrealistic expectations lead to unnecessary anxieties.

Forgive everybody. They have taken up the onerous task of living with themselves.

If lines were written to be read,
why is there a reason to read between the lines?

Nobody can be you, no matter how hard they try.
You cannot be anybody else, no matter how hard you try.

Pick up a rock and try to smooth it by pouring water over it.
Then walk to a stream and pick up a pebble along the shore.

What is your legacy?

Think about it long enough, and you will become it.

Don't worry about not being famous.
Enjoy your anonymity; it's precious (ask any celebrity).

If you are capable of deep depression, you are also capable of great happiness. Just flip the switch the other way.

Abandon yourself to God.

You cannot solve a major problem by approaching it in the same plane—you need a complete paradigm shift.

What is in your destiny will happen. If you choose to change it, that's because your destiny wants you to.

Before you give up on something,
make sure you gave it its adequate learning curve.

We are able to easily recognize faults in others because we are already familiar with them in ourselves.

Everybody is important. Nobody is *in*dispensable.

In the end, your fingerprint will be unique
because of what good you left behind.

Your best friend is you. Your worst enemy is also you.

If you have basic needs, good health, peace of mind,
and family and friends, you have no reason
to complain or be unhappy.

Nobody is incapable of change.
Some just take longer than others.

My desires are the cause of my suffering.

Faith and science are not contradictions—
faith is one way for spirituality; science is another.

Knowledge is power. Ignorance is bliss.

The only constant thing in the world is change.

Obsession is the mother of perfection.

No information is useless.

If, and only if, you can do everything that another person does and more, are you superior to that person. You are not better because you do things *you think* are superior to what the other person does.

When force does not work, try gentleness.

Nobody is perfect. Nobody is nothing.

I am merely a spectator of God's events
unfolding in front of me.

A single thought can change your entire life.

Let go of everything in your mind for a few moments.
Think of you as a continuum of the universe.
Experience the release that comes from it.

There is no rule without an exception. Including this one.

If there is one goal to work for in life, it is finding God.
If there is another, it is finding yourself.

The mind is finite. Let it hold small thoughts—
and there will be no room for grand ideas.

I have started nothing. I have ended nothing.
I am merely a medium through which everything flows.

We must be primed first before we can accept change.
How and when and if that priming happens,
is a matter of destiny.

External things do not provoke desire.
It is the internal desire that searches for external things.

Under any set of circumstances, stagnant or changing, a person will respond based on his unique set of genes. If everybody realizes this, there will be more understanding and less conflict.

The sooner you realize that God is in charge and not you, the sooner you will be at peace.

You don't choose your destiny—your destiny chooses you.

Challenge your beliefs. Shake them to their core. Every single one of them. You will be surprised to see how many of them were so wrong.

Pleasure is fleeting; suffering, constant.

No book can be written for others to read. It is written by a man for himself. If others want to look into it, they can. If a book becomes memorable, it is due neither to the greatness of the author nor to the receptivity of the audience; but to the magic of the Creator Himself, who made all such hearts beat as one.

Things don't get better with time—time *is* the healer.

The world presents you with snapshots of people; when what you should be getting is their videos, both before and after. It's not fair.

Every moment of life is an accident—
a miracle how things are well.

To truly experience sound, you should be blind.

The only approach to life is a philosophical one—
any other, and you are out of peace.

When people are talking about their problems,
what they are really talking about is their fears.

The ignorant man is happier than the learned, simply because he comprehends forces beyond his nature and is more accepting of things uncomfortable. The learned man, on the other hand, is cursed to find explanations, fearful of the mystical, and a slave of his anxiety.

Don't dwell on the scarcity of man—
look at the abundance of God.

If everything is happening for a reason,
what is not happening is also not happening for a reason.

My mind restless; my body, helpless.

The feeling of being wronged by others, while at the same time not being wrong, is an almost universal one.

Nothing is so subtle, so imperceptible, so fleeting, as a thought. Nothing has so much power to change the world either.

The moment you open your eyes, you are looking outward. I wish God gave us another set of eyes that when open, look inward.

Do not be disappointed if the other person does not like what you like. It is also okay for you to not like what the other person likes.

Start talking in terms of "my body does not want to cooperate," "my mind is confused," or "my heart says I should do it." This way you will isolate your real self, your soul, from the physical elements- mind, heart, and body. The soul is the truth, the real "I".

Make God a habit.

Throughout the course of life, at several points, you will have to assume, even though it is false, that you know more than the other person, who in reality, knows a lot more than you do but just doesn't appear that way. Otherwise, you cannot move ahead in life.

All thoughts are rediscoveries.

On true communication.

The subconscious of one person communicates with the subconscious of another person. This communication, of which both of us are unaware, is more important than what we consciously say to each other.

So, if we are in our hearts, humble and honest, and truly concerned about the good of the other person (and this may be hard to acquire as a habit), these vibes are picked up by the subconscious of the other person, and lead to a fruitful exchange.

You may be struggling to know who you are. Here is a simple way. What you *do* shows you who you are.

It is not fair that God made such complex creatures as humans and left them to interact with one another without proper training on how to do so.

While not being apparent during the reign of torment, the benefit of that suffering is realized decades down the road.

Very rarely is a person's image of himself a true reflection of his real state of affairs; it is usually some elevated state where he wants to be. So, be careful when you talk to people—while you think you are addressing this person you see in front of you, your words are actually reaching the elevated self of that person.

You only live once, so you have to get it right the first time.

Man does something only when all these five things are satisfied—he must be able to do it, willing to do it, be in the right mood to do it; and it must align with what he believes, and protect his ego.

It is unfair that God made man's thoughts, capacities, and energies invisible by limiting his body by the skin.

Man has a tendency to always find something he cannot acquire, and spend his life brooding about it. This, perhaps, is what keeps men occupied and moves them in their life. For acquiring that something means no more movement, or stillness.

There are two types of people in this world—
one is me, the other is everybody else.

Pleasure is palpable by its presence;
nonsuffering is inconspicuous by the absence of affliction.

Everything happens by God's will. This thought has freed me from several things—sympathizing with the unfortunate to the point of depressing myself; blaming others for doing bad things or not doing enough good; blaming myself for all the things I did and didn't do; and jealousy, because God chooses to give His gifts as He pleases.

Not everybody is an intellectual.
But everybody has feelings.

If you know God, it's easy to decipher the codes He has for your life. If you can't decipher these codes, life will be very confusing.

A hundred people can look at a single scenario, and draw a hundred different conclusions from it. Some people get it; some people don't.

People who run after things are of two types—one, people who haven't found what they want; and two, people who have found what they want, but don't know that they did.

Every day of my life, I regret the way I lived yesterday.

## On reading books.

Books on religion or philosophy do not give away the essence of their message. They want you to work very hard, and dig up the gems that are hidden in the pile of rocks that makes up the bulk of the book. It is not easy. When you pick up a stone, you have to look at it very carefully, think about it, and analyze it to see if it is a rock worth discarding or a gem worth keeping in your heart always and applying it to your daily life. No doubt, there are a few gems in every rock pile, but the digging is for you to do.

As an adult, you have to look back upon your childhood and analyze how it has been, even though you feel it has been perfect. There may be things that you grew up with, that you are not aware of as an adult, such as some attitudes, ways of doing things, fears. Then, you can unlearn at least some of the things that were part of you as a child. This you do consciously and with full awareness, and this is when you will be reborn as an adult.

Do not expect a lot from a person. He or she has several people as part of his or her life—the fact that you are getting some attention at all is something you should be happy about.

Great accomplishments of some are due to great sacrifices by others.

Reason kills, faith heals. Pick one.

There are two sides to every single thing—
positive and negative.
One of the main reasons for conflict between people is that while one approaches a given situation from a history of positive experience, the other approaches the same with a history of negative experience. These feelings are not overt, they are always subliminal and underlie all conflicts.

What things would you do—or not do—
if it weren't for others?

Hoarding wealth is a crime against humanity.

Are you living a life avoiding superiors, conflicting with equals, and tyrannizing your subordinates?

Every single one of us has a feeling of how things are supposed to be—people, circumstances. These feelings become part of us during our growth, and are subconscious. We are not usually aware of them, until they show up in our reactions to people and events. If a person or a situation does not fit our image, we are thrown off balance, and struggle to find our bearings again.

When you forgive others, you are not doing them a favor; you are doing yourself one.

When God gives you only a few things, or only a little of something, He is actually doing you a favor, by allowing you to relish those things even more. Think about it—if you could have *anything* in the world you want, and as *much* as you want, would you enjoy it in the same way?

Man causes more miseries to man than nature does. More poverty, disease, and anguish are caused by man's direct cruelty, or greed to accumulate, or by withholding help than nature can ever hope to surpass.

The wise man knows himself and the ignorant.
The ignorant knows neither.

Are you full of enthusiasm to influence people to a better way of life? Are you trying to find somebody who will listen to your suggestions? How about starting with somebody you know very well—you! (You will be surprised to see how resistant that 'you' is to your proposed changes!)

While trying to become somebody in life, do not forget to spend time with your family and friends. Whether you become that somebody or not, you will not have missed out on what matters most in life.

If you start focusing on the accolades bestowed upon you by people, at some point in life, you will realize that those were all meaningless and even worthy of discarding. By that time, it would have been too late to start focusing on yourself and your inner spirit. My suggestion is that you get started early in life on your values, thoughts, and spiritual growth. In the end, you will have such fulfillment in your life that no amount of money or fame would have sufficed to equal.

Fortunate is the man who has limits on his perspective, for everything under it is fully available for him to enjoy.

How would you know the unwritten rules of life?

For each response that comes from you to any situation, think—is it my *feeling* or my *reason* that is responding this way? Is this good in the short term (response by feeling) or in the long term (response by reason)?

A lot of rich and famous people eventually end up in spirituality. So, if you have not become rich or famous, cheer up; you have gotten a shortcut to spirituality. You don't have to go through all the hard work and heartaches of trying and becoming rich and famous—a materialistic and short-lived phase. Instead, you can spend all that energy and time trying to become spiritual, which will last forever.

Some people appear stupid,
because their agendas are unknown to you.

Sometimes you look around everywhere for an answer.
You don't find it because you haven't looked
right under your nose.

If you associate yourself with morons,
you will bear the consequences.

On true freedom.

When seeking freedom, most people are thinking
financial, political, or religious freedom.
But real freedom is freedom from these-

Fear—
Imagine a life where you don't have to be afraid of anything.

Desire—
Imagine a life free from the desires that hold you prisoner.

Anger—
Imagine a life where you are at peace at all times.

Science, in its overzealousness, thinks it is explaining the *why*, when it is merely explaining the *how*.

All philosophers' lives are filled with pain, either physical or emotional or spiritual. The pain is not severe enough to kill them, but leaves them constantly restless, thoughtful. Knowing not what else to do, they write.

The greatest evidence of destiny—
the inability of people to learn from their mistakes.

The ultimate goal.

The goal you should aim for should be no less than the ultimate one—that of becoming God Himself. Any other goal of riches or fame is less than that. By becoming God, I don't mean becoming omnipotent or omnipresent, but becoming a manifestation of wisdom, kindness, and love.

How is your health? Not good.
How are your thoughts? Not good.
Okay, let's change the thoughts to good,
and we'll see if the health changes as well or not…

Thank God I'm not in charge.

Were it not for suffering,
how would I ever think about life?

You will be shown your place in the world.

People who have wronged have the ability to forgive.

Do not compare yourself with how you were ten years ago as far as money, fame, power. The comparison should be how much more spiritually evolved you are.

Learn to recognize your moods.

The philosophical idea behind having two eyes and seeing only one object may be this: when you see two different things, good and bad—see them as one—meaning, react to them the same way. I know it is hard to respond to pain the same way we respond to pleasure, but if we understand that there is but one force behind both, we probably will be able to handle pain better, and not get too carried away by pleasure.

It is to be recognized that fame, while pursued by some people with great effort, is sometimes thrust upon other people against their will.

The reason I am not bored is I think about things that are different each day, not things that are the same.

Experience is the greatest teacher, but also the most expensive one.

There are two main types of people—those who enter life completely unprepared, and those who enter it with completely wrong theories, attitudes, and beliefs. A third type, those who enter prepared and with the right attitude, are truly rare.

## A patient's appeal.

I have come to seek your help, because you are more
knowledgeable than me. By showing up at your doorstep,
I have already admitted that fact. So please be kind
in your words and in the tone of your voice.

I may be interested in my health, or I may not,
but the fact that I am here today shows I care.
So please show me some consideration.

I may not be as educated as you, but I know enough
to come to you when something is not right.
So please treat me with dignity.

I am concerned about what has happened to me,
and because it is my body and not yours,
please explain to me in my language so I can understand.

I have traveled a distance to come to you, and waited a long time to talk to you. I know your time is valuable, but so is the time I spend to care for my health. So please make me feel comfortable.

If I ask you the same question several times, it is because I don't understand what you said. Or it is too hard for me to bear the bad news. Or it is expensive, inconvenient, or causes hardship to my family. Or I may not have heard you right, because I am sick, in pain, and have not slept in days. So please be patient with me.

On asking others of things you want.

There are certain things a person will not give you no matter what. Some things he doesn't care much for, he will give you, but only if you ask him nicely. Some things he was going to throw away anyway, but your way of asking for them will make him not give them to you. Only among really close friends can you ask for something and just get it, but it still helps to be nice, because you don't know what mood your friend is in when you ask him.

What is amazing is not man's unawareness of God, but how
he has successfully managed to severely narrow his vision to
the ordinary material things of life—
while overlooking the abundant sunshine,
fresh air, giant trees, and the earth he walks upon,
all of which literally blind him with God's presence.

I don't know if everything is predestined or not, but no other thought has given me more peace than believing it is.

What am I doing here, grabbing every moment from the future and pushing it into the past?

CPSIA information can be obtained at www.ICGtesting.com
Printed in the USA
LVOW06s1533091214

418010LV00001B/125/P

9 780692 026458